Dedication

To all those who ever struggled with learning a foreign language
and to Wolfgang Karfunkel

CONVERSATIONAL HEBREW QUICK AND EASY

The Most Innovative Technique
To Learn the Hebrew Language

Part - 1

YATIR NITZANY

Foreword

For many years I struggled to learn Spanish, and I still knew no more than about twenty words. Consequently, I was extremely frustrated. One day I stumbled upon this method as I was playing around with word combinations. Suddenly, I came to the realization that every language has a certain core group of words that are most commonly used and, simply by learning them, one could gain the ability to engage in quick and easy conversational Spanish.

I discovered which words those were, and I narrowed them down to three hundred and fifty that, once memorized, one could connect and create one's own sentences. The variations were and are *infinite*! By using this incredibly simple technique, I could converse at a proficient level and speak Spanish. Within a week, I astonished my Spanish-speaking friends with my newfound ability. The next semester I registered at my university for a Spanish language course, and I applied the same principles I had learned in that class (grammar, additional vocabulary, future and past tense, etc.) to those three hundred and fifty words I already had memorized, and immediately I felt as if I had grown wings and learned how to fly.

At the end of the semester, we took a class trip to San José, Costa Rica. I was like a fish in water, while the rest of my classmates were floundering and still struggling to converse. Throughout the following months, I again applied the same principle to other languages—French, Portuguese, Italian, and Arabic, all of which I now speak proficiently, thanks to this very simple technique.

This method is by far the fastest way to master quick and easy conversational language skills. There is no other technique that compares to my concept. It is effective, it worked for me, and it will work for you. Just be consistent with my program. By learning these mere 350 words, which I will teach you in this book, you too will also succeed the way I and many, many others have. This book is *not* a grammar book, nor a phrasebook, it's purely meant to assist in aiding you to communicate in a foreign language.

Contents

Introduction to Hebrew.................................... 6

Hebrew Grammar and Pronunciation...........................8

The Program.....................................11

Building Bridges................................49

Useful Vocabulary in Hebrew..........................60

Note from the Author.....................................64

Also by Yatir Nitzany.....................................65

THE HEBREW LANGUAGE

The two most ancient written cultures in the world (other than Egyptian with its hieroglyphics) are Chinese in the Far East and Hebrew in the Middle East. Abraham, the father of the three monotheistic faiths, was the first person to speak Hebrew, and the book to introduce his story is the Bible. This awesome literary work covers thousands of years of history, and the book is translated into 126 languages. Hebrew further developed from generation to generation, and its vocabulary became more extensive.

For three millenniums, great works of Hebrew scholars were written in Hebrew and translated into many languages; works such as the Mishna, Talmud, Haggadah, and Derash.

Great philosophers, such as Saadia Gaon (around 800 C.E.) and Rabbi Moses Ben Maimon—known as Maimonides—in the twelfth century, also wrote their philosophies in Hebrew and Arabic (the lingua franca of this historical period). Their works were then translated into Latin and many other languages.

In the medieval era, there were well-known scholars, poets, and authors in Spain, such as Yehuda Halevy, Iben Ezra, Iben Gavirol, and a large number of other writers who expressed themselves in Hebrew.

The Torah, known as the Five Books of Moses in the Bible, was translated into a more comprehensive Hebrew with commentaries by Rashi (a famous rabbi). His native language was French.

In the Enlightenment era, since the great Jewish philosopher Moses Mendelssohn, as well the national poet of Israel, Hayim Nechman Bialik, who expressed himself in the most eloquent Hebrew, creating and adopting it into a modern language and creating new words. Ben Yehuda, who wrote the modern Hebrew dictionary, together with hundreds of writers and superb poets, such as Shaul Tchernichovsky, left an exquisite legacy of literary works in Hebrew. Yet for none of them, Hebrew was their mother tongue. At that time, the language was considered a dead language.

In 1969, Shay Agnon was awarded the Nobel Prize in literature. He wrote in Hebrew, and most of his books are translated into many other languages.

In America, from the Pilgrims' times until 1929, no student was accepted into any Ivy League University, such as Harvard or Yale, unless they read and wrote Hebrew. Most Ivy League universities in the US have a Hebrew Department for Biblical history and the literature of Hebrew scripts. Nowadays, even at the Universities of Tokyo in Japan and Seoul in South Korea, there are Hebrew departments where Hebrew is taught.

In Israel, where the Hebrew language is the national language, there is the Academy of the Hebrew Language, which assists new learners of the language anytime.

HEBREW GRAMMAR AND PRONUNCIATIONS

Accents of the Hebrew Language

*For Middle Eastern languages, including Hebrew, Arabic, Farsi, Pashto, Urdu, Hindi, etc., and also German, to properly pronounce the *kh* or *ch* is essential, for example, *Chanukah* (a Jewish holiday) or *Khaled* (a Muslim name) or *Nacht* ("night" in German). The best way to describe *kh* or *ch* is to say "ka" or "ha" while at the same time putting your tongue at the back of your throat and blowing air. It's pronounced similarly to the sound that you make while clearing your throat of phlegm.

*In Hebrew, the accent *aayin* is pronounced as 'aa, and is pronounced deep at the back of your throat, rather similar to the sound one would make when gagging. In the program, the symbol for *ayin* is '*aa* or '*oo*.

Ha is pronounced as "ha." Pronunciation takes place deep at the back of your throat, and for correct pronunciation one must constrict the back of the throat and exhale air while simultaneously saying "ha." In the program, this strong *h* ("ha") is emphasized whenever *ah*, *ha*, *eh*, *he*, and *oh* is encountered.

Please keep all these in mind whenever you come across any of these accents in the program.

Basic Grammar which you will Encounter in the Program

*In the Hebrew language, adjectives come after the noun, for example, "sunglasses" - מׁשקפיים / *Mishkafaei* - מׁשקפי ("glasses").*Shemesh* - שמׁש ("sun"). The same rule also applies for possessive adjectives. For example, "your" / *shelcha* / שלך; "my" / *sheli* / שלי; and "his" or "hers" / *sehlo* - שלו or *shela*- שלה, etc., will always follow the noun, and the article "the" / *ha* / ה... will always precede the noun. For example:

* "your office" / *Ha*- ה ("the") *misrad* - משרד ("office") *shelcha* - שלך("your")

* "his house" / *Ha* - ה ("the") *ba-it* - בית("house") *shelo* - שלו ("his")

* "my place" / *Ha* - ה ("the") *makom* - מקום ("place") *sheli* - שלי("my")

*The word *et* - את in the Hebrew language is a term which is used in order to indicate a definite or direct object, but it depends on how it is used in a sentence. *Et* doesn't directly translate into the English language. So to say "I read," you would say, *Ani Koreh* - אני קורא. To say "I read the book," you would say, *Ani Koreh et ha'sefer* - אני קורא את הספר. Because *sefer* - ספר ("book") is definite and the direct object, you need both the *et* and the *ha*-. *Et* doesn't have to be followed by a "the" suffix *ha*- ("the") when it is definite without the *ha*-. Such cases include names, so *Ani Koreh Et Shakespeare* - אני קורא את שייקספיר would be "I read Shakespeare." *Et* is also very commonly used when describing "that," for example, "I want that" would be *ani rotze et ze* - אני רוצה את זה. Just keep in mind that *et* is actually a preposition wthat is placed before any definite direct object.

*In Hebrew, "because" / *biglal* - בגלל is always followed by "that" / *shae* - ש.... For example, "because I go" is *biglal shae ani olech* - בגלל שאני הולך.

*In Hebrew, the article *"a"* doesn't exist. For example, in the English language "a book" in Hebrew would translate to *sefer* - ספר.

The Program

Another example is "I want to buy a house" / *ani* ("I") - אני *rotze* ("want") - רוצה *liknot* ("to buy") - לקנות *beit* ("house")- בית.

*In the English language, first person verbs usually begin with "I am" and end with *-ing*. However, in Hebrew there is no *-ing*,and there is no "am." There is just "I," *ani* - אני. So "I am going" is "*Ani olech*" - אני הולך.

*Also, in Hebrew, "you're" is *ata* - אתה. There is no "are"; there is only "you," *ata*. Though there is "are you," *ha'iim ata* - האם אתה.

*In Hebrew grammar, gender is always used. In Hebrew, every noun is either masculine or feminine and sometimes both. In this program, whenever you encounter (m.), it will signify "masculine," and (f.) will signify "feminine."

*In Hebrew, in relation to compound words, the article precedes the second word. "Where is **the** train station?" / *eifo tachanat* **ha**rakevet? / איפה התחנת רכבת?

*In Hebrew regarding a statement with the definite article of a noun, the article precedes the adjective as well.
For example:
"where is **the** public transportation?" / *eifo* **ha** *tachbura* **ha** *tziburit?* / איפה התחנה הציבורית?

*In hebrew to signify "and" we use *ve* - ו... or *oo* - או. Any word beginning with *b, v, m, p,* or *f* prior to them *ve* - ו.. / "and" will become *oo* - או...
Gan **oo** *vait* / "garden **and** house" / גן ובית

The Program

I / I am – Ani - אני

With you - (male) Itch'a - אִתְּךָ

With you - (female) It'ach - אִתָּךְ

With us – Itanu - איתנו

With – Eem - עם

For you - (m) Bishvilcha - בשבילך

For you - (f)bishvilech - בשבילך

You, you are - (M) Atta - אתה

You, you are - (M) (F) ah'tt - את

Are you - (m) Ha'iim atta – האם אתה

Are you - (f) Ha'iim ah'tt – האם את

From – Me – מ...

Sentences composed from the vocabulary you just learned"

Are you from Israel?
(Male) Ha'iim ata/ (female) a'tt mi isra'el?
האם אתה\את מישראל?

I am from Jerusalem.
Ani mi yerushalaym.
אני מירושלים.

I am with you.
(M)Ani it'cha/ (F)it'ach.
אני איתך\איתך.

This is for you.
(m)Zeh bishvilcha/ (f)bishvilech.
זה בשבילך\בשבילך .

*In Hebrew, "are you" is *ha'iim atta -* / *ah'tt – את \ האם אתה.*
However, when using "is" or "are" as the present plural form of
the verb "to be," such as "you are" / *atta, ah'tt – את, אתה;* "he/she
is" / *hu, hee – היא, הוא;* "they are" / *hem, hen – הן, הם*, the "is/are" is
omitted from the pronoun or noun. * "He is at home" / *hu beh
bayit – בבית הוא,* "the boys are here" / *ha yeladim poe – הילדים פה.*

11

With him - It-o - איתו
With her - It-a - איתה
This (or) **this is - (M)**Zeh - זה
This (or) **this is - (F)**zot - זאת
Without him – Biladav - בלעדיו
Without them - (m) Bila'day'hem - בלעדיהם
Without them - (f)bila'day'hen - בלעדיהן
Always – Tamid - תמיד
At the (or) In - (Male) Beh – ב...
At the (or) In - (Female) ba – בה...
Sometimes – Lefamim - לפעמים
Maybe - Oo'lai - אולי
Maybe - itachen - היתכן
Today – Hayom - היום
He (or) **he is –** Hu - הוא
She (or) **she is –** Hee - היא

Are you at the house?
Ha'eem ata ba ba'iit?
האם אתה בבית?

I am always with her.
Ani tamid ita.
אני תמיד איתה.

Are you alone today?
Ha'eem ata levad hayom?
האם אתה לבד היום?

Sometimes I go without him.
Lifa'ameem ani olech biladav.
לפעמים אני הולך בלעדיו.

12

Was - Haya היה
I was - Ani hayiti - הייתי
To be - Li-hiyote - להיות
Good – Tov - טוב
Here – Poe - פה
Here - Kan כאן
Here - Hena הנה
Very - Mei'od - מאוד
And – Ve – ו...
Between – Ben - בין
If – Eim - אם
Now - Ka'et / Achshav – עכשיו \ כעת
Tomorrow – Machar - מחר

I was here with them.
Ani hayiti poe itam.
אני הייתי פה איתם.

You and I.
Ata/ah'tt ve ani.
אתה\את ואני.

I was home at 5pm.
Ha'yti ba ba'eet bei sha'a chamesh achar atzorhaim.
הייתי בבית בשעה חמש אחר הצהריים.

Between now and tomorrow.
Bein achshav lemachar.
בין עכשיו למחר.

This is for us.
Ze bishvileinoo.
זה בשבילנו.

*In Hebrew, when the subject of the sentence is definite, then any nouns, adjectives, or determiners must have *ha – ה*...placed before them. The only exceptions are relative clauses and prepositions, for example, "your son" / *ha'ben shelach –* הבן שלך and "the boy is in school" *ha'yeled beh beit ha'sefer –* הילד בבית הספר.

13

The – Ha – ה...
A (article) - No equivalent
Same - Oto ha'davar אותו הדבר
Later - Achar-kach אחר כך
Later - yoter meuchar יותר מאוחר
Yes – Ken - כן
Happy - Sam'eiach - שמח
To – Li – ל...
Better - Yoter-tov יותר טוב
preferable - Adif עדיף
Then – Az - אז
Also / too / as well – Gam גם
Also / too / as well – Gam kan גם כן
Very - Mei'od - מאוד

It's better to be home later.
Yoter tov leeh'yot ba ba'yeet mehochar yoter.
יותר טוב להיות בבית מאוחר יותר

If this is good, then I am happy.
Eem ze tov, az ani sam'ei'ach.
אם זה טוב, אז אני שמח.

Yes, you are very good.
(Male) Ken, ata tov mei'od.
כן, אתה טוב מאוד.

Yes, you are very good.
(Female) Ken, att tova mei'od.
כן, את טובה מאוד.

The same day.
Oto ha-yom.
אותו היום.

  *This *isn't* a phrase book! The purpose of this book is *solely* to provide you with the tools to create *your own* sentences!

14

Ok – Beseder - בסדר

Even if - Afilu im אפילו אם / **Even if -** Lamrot – למרות

Afterwards – Acharei אחרי

Afterwards – Achar kach – אחר כך

After – Acharei - אחרי

Worse - Garo'aa - גרוע

Where - Eifo איפה

Where - Heychan – היכן

Everything - ha'kol הכל / **Anything -** Kol davar כל דבר

Somewhere - Eifo shh 'hu איפשהו

Somewhere - Hey chan shh 'hu – היכנשהו

What – Ma - מה

Almost – Kimaat - כמעט

There – Sham - שם

Afterwards is worse.
Acharkach zeh yoter garo'aa.
אחר כך זה יותר גרוע.

Even if I go now.
(m)Afilu im ani holech/(f)holechet achshav.
אפילו אם אני הולך\הולכת עכשיו.

Where is everything?
Heychan kol-davar?
היכן כל דבר?

Maybe somewhere.
Oolai heychan shh'hu.
אולי היכנשהו.

What? I am almost there.
Mah? Ani kimat sham.
מה? אני כמעט שם.

Where are you?
Eifo ata/ah'tt?
איפה אתה\את?

The Program

Good morning - Boker tov – בוקר טוב
How are you - (m) Ma'shlomcha - מה שלומך
How are you - (f) Ma'shlomech- מה שלומך
Without us - Bila'dei'nu - בלעדינו
Hello – Shalom - שלום
What is your name - (m) Ma shimcha - מה שמך
What is your name - (f) Ma shmech - מה שמך
How old are you - (m) Ben kama ata- בן כמה אתה
How old are you - (f) Bat kama ah'tt – בת כמה את
Already – Kvar - כבר
Son - Ben בן
Daughter - Baat – בת
Still - Ad'aain - עדיין
House - Ba'itt - בית
Car – Mechoniit - מכונית

Good morning, how are you today?
Boker tov, ma'shlomcha/ma'shlomech hayom?
בוקר טוב, מה שלומך \ מה שלומך היום?

Hello, what is your name?
Shalom, ma shimcha/shmech?
שלום, מה שמך\מה שמך?

How old are you?
Ben kama ata/bat kama ah'tt?
בן כמה אתה\בת כמה את?

Where are you from?
Mi eifo ata/att?
מאיפה אתה\את?

She is not in the car, so maybe she is still at the house?
Hee lo ba mechoniit, az oo'lai hee ad'aain ba-ba'itt?
היא לא במכונית, אז אולי היא עדיין בבית?

I am in the car already with your son and daughter.
Ani kvar ba mechoniit eim ha ben ve ha baat shelach.
אני כבר במכונית עם הבן והבת שלך.

Thank you – Todah - תודה
For – Bishvil - בשביל
That (or) **that is - (m)** Zeh זה
That (or) **that is - (f)** Zot – זאת
It is – Zeh - זה
Time – Zman - זמן
No / not – Lo - לא
Late – Meuchar - מאוחר
Away - (m) Rachok רחוק
Away - (f)rechoka – רחוקה
Similar – Domeh - דומה
To go – Llalechet - ללכת
Almost - Kim'aat - כמעט

Thank you Yossi.
Toda lecha Yossi.
.תודה לך יוסי

It is almost time to go.
Zeh kimat ha z'man lalechet.
.זה כמעט הזמן ללכת

I am not here, I am away.
Ani lo poe, ani rachok/rechoka.
.אני לא פה, אני רחוק\רחוקה

That house is similar to ours.
Ha ba'iit hazei dom'ae leshelanu.
.הבית הזה דומה לשלנו

*In Hebrew, there are three ways of describing time:
Zman - זמן / "era": "this isn't the right time" / *ze lo ha-zman
ha'mat'him –* זה לא הזמן המתאים
Pa'am (singular) - פעם / *pa'mim -* פעמים (plural): "first time" / *pa'am
harishona –* פעם הראשונה or "three times" / *shalosh pa'amim –* שלוש
פעמים.
Sha'ha - שעה / "hour": "What time is it?" / *Ma ha'sha'ha?* - מה
השעה?

Other - Acher אחר
Other - Shonei שונה
Side – Tzad - צד
Until – Ad - עד
Yesterday – Etmol - אתמול
Without - Bl'ee בלי
Without - Le'lo ללא
Since – Meaz - מאז
Day – Yom - יום
Before – Lifnei - לפני
But - Aval אבל
Hard – Kasheh - קשה
Impossible - Bilti'efshari – בלתי אפשרי
However - Oolam – אולם

I am from the other side.
Ani mae hatsad ha shainee.
אני מהצד השני.

But I was here until late yesterday.
Aval ani ha'yitti poe aa'd meuchar etmol.
אבל אני הייתי פה עד מאוחר אתמול.

The coffee is without sugar.
Ha'kafei bl'ee sucar.
הקפה בלי סוכר.

This is very hard, but it's not impossible.
Zeh mei'od kasheh, aval ze lo bilti'efshari
זה מאוד קשה, אבל זה לא בלתי אפשרי.

*This *isn't* a phrase book! The purpose of this book is *solely* to provide you with the tools to create *your own* sentences!

18

I say / I am saying - (m) Ani omer - אני אומר
I say / I am saying - (f) Ani omeret - אני אומרת
I want - (m) Ani rotzeh - אני רוֹצֶה
I want - (f) Ani rotza –אני רוֹצָה
I go / I am going - (m) Ani holech - אני הולך
I go / I am going - (f) Ani holechet – אני הולכת
I need - (m) Ani tza'rich - אני צריך
I need - (f) Ani tz'rei'cha – אני צריכה
I see / I am seeing - (M) Ani ro'eh - אני רוֹאֶה
I see / I am seeing - (F) Ani ro'ha – אני רוֹאָה
To see - Li-rote - לראות
Everywhere - Bechol makom – בכל מקום
My – Sheli - שלי

I am saying no!
Ani omer/omeret lo!
!אני אומר\אומרת לֹא

You need to be at home.
Ata tzarich leeh'yot ba ba'yeet.
.אתה צריך להיות בבית

I see light outside.
Ani ro'eh/ro'ha orr bachutz.
.אני רוֹאֶה\רוֹאָה אור בחוץ

What time is it right now?
Ma ha'sha'ha achshav?
?מה השעה עכשיו

I see this everywhere.
Ani ro'eh/ro'ha et ze bechol makom.
.אני רוֹאֶה\רוֹאָה את זה בכל מקום

*In the English language, first person verbs usually begin with "I am" and end with -*ing*. However, in Hebrew there is no -*ing*,and there is no "am." There is just "I," *ani -* אני. So "I am going" is "*Ani olech –* אני הולך."

19

Without you - (M)biladecha –בִּלְעָדֶיךָ
Without you - (F)bila'daeich - בִּלְעָדַיִךְ
Cousin - (M) Ben dode – בן דוד
Cousin - (F) bat doda – בת דודה
Happy - (M) Samae'ach - שמח
Cousin - (F)smecha - שמחה
Easy – Kal - קל
Night – Laila - לילה
Light – Orr - אור
Outside - Hachutza החוצה
Outside - bachutz – בחוץ
To – Li – ל...
To sell – Limkor - למכור
That – Sheh – ש...
That he is - (m)sheh hu - שהוא
That she is – (f)sheh he - שהיא

I want to see this in the day.
Ani rotzeh/rotza lir-ote et ze ba yom.
אני רוֹצֶה\רוֹצָה לראות את זה ביום

I am happy to be here without my cousin.
Ani samae'ach/smecha li-hiyot poe b'lee haben-dod sheli.
אני שמח\שמחה להיות פה בלי הבן דוד שלי.

I need to be there at night.
Ani tza'rich/tz'rei'cha li-hiyot sham ba-laila.
אני צריך\צריכה להיות שם בלילה.

Is it easy to sell this table?
Haiim kal limkor et hasholchan ha ze?
האם קל למכור את השולחן הזה?

I need to know that that is a good idea.
Ani tzarich/tzraicha lada'aat sheh ze ra'aayon tov.
אני צריך לדעת שזה רעיון טוב.

*In the last sentence, we use "that" as a conjunction *(sheh – ש...)*
and a demonstrative pronoun *(ze)*.

Place – Makom - מקום
To find – Limtzo - למצוא
To look - Le-histakel - להסתכל
To look for / to search – Lechapes - לחפש
Near, close - Al yad ליד
Near, close - karov – קרוב
To use - Le-hishtamesh - להשתמש
To know - La-da'aat - לדעת
To decide - Le-hachlit - להחליט
To wait – Lechakot - לחכות
Book – Sefer - ספר

This place is easy to find.
Kal limtzo et hamakom hazeh.
קל למצוא את המקום הזה.

I am saying to wait until tomorrow.
Ani omer/omeret lechakote aa'd machar.
אני אומר\אומרת לחכות עד מחר.

I want to use this.
Ani rotzeh/rotza le-hishtamesh be zeh.
אני רוֹצֶה\ רוֹצָה להשתמש בזה.

Is it possible to look for this book in the library?
Efshar lechapes et ha sefer ba sifriya?
אפשר לחפש את הספר בספריה?

Is this place near?
Ha'eem ha makom hazei karov?
האם המקום הזה קרוב?

I want to know where is the grocery store.
Ani rotzeh/rotza lada'aat heychan chanut ha-makolet.
אני רוֹצֶה\ רוֹצָה לדעת היכן חנות המכולת.

Because - Mekeivan sheh ש מכיוון...
Because - biglal sheh ש בגלל...
Because - Ki כי
Them / They - (M)Hem - הם
Them / They - (F) Hen - הן
Their - (M) Shela-hem - שלהם
Their - (F)shelahen - שלהן
Mine – Sheli - שלי
To understand – Lehaveen - להבין
Problem - Be'aya בעיה
Problems - Be'ayot בעיות
I can – Ani (m)yachol – אני יכול
I can – Ani (f)yechola – יכולה
Can I? – Ha'iim ani (m) yachol? האם אני יכול?
Can I? – Ha'iim ani (f)yechola? – האם אני יכולה?
I do / I am doing - (m)Ani oseh – אני עוֹשֶׂה
I do / I am doing - (f)Ani Osa – אני עוֹשָׂה

I can work today.
Ani yachol la'avod hayoum.
אני יכול לעבוד היום.

I do what I want.
Ani o'sae ma shae ani rotzei.
אני עושה מה שאני רוצה.

That book is mine.
Ha sefer ha ze sheli.
הספר הזה שלי.

I have to understand the problem.
Ani tza'rich/tz'rei'cha le-haveen et ha be'aya.
אני צריך\צריכה להבין את הבעיה.

*In Hebrew, "because" / *biglal* – בגלל (or) *mekeivan* - מכיוון is always followed by "that" / *shae* – ש.... For example, "because I go" is *biglal shae ani olech*- בגלל שאני הולך (or) *mekeivan shae ani olech* – מכיוון שאני הולך.

Food - Ochel / mazon – מזון \ אוכל
Water – Maiim - מים
Hotel - Malon / Beit-malon – בית מלון \ מלון
View – Nof - נוף
There are/ there is – Yesh - יש
Much, many, a lot – Harbei - הרבה
A little – Ktzat - קצת
Both - Shnay-hem - שניהם
To buy – Liknot - לקנות
Two – Shnaim - שניים
Between – Ben - בן
Both – Shnei - שני

There are many tourists in Israel every summer.
Yesh harbei tayarim be Israel kol ka'itz.
יש הרבה תיירים בישראל כל קיץ.

I like this hotel because it's near the beach.
Ani ohev et ha malon hazei kee hoo nimtza le'yad ha chof.
אני אוהב את המלון הזה כי הוא נמצא ליד החוף.

I want to look at the view.
Ani rotzei leheestakel al ha nof.
אני רוצה להסתכל על הנוף.

I want to buy a water bottle.
Ani rotze/rotza liknot bakbok mayim.
אני רוֹצֶה\רוֹצָה לקנות בקבוק מים.

I see the view of the city from my hotel room.
Ani ro'eh et ha nof shel ha irr mi chadar ha malon sheli.
אני רואה את הנוף של העיר מחדר המלון שלי.

I need to decide between both places.
Ani tza'rich/tz'rei'cha le-hachlit ben shnai ha'mekomot.
אני צריך\צריכה להחליט בן שני מקומות.

I am very happy to know that everything is ok.
Ani mei'od samae'ach la-da'aat shae hakol beseder.
אני מאוד שמח לדעת שהכל בסדר

Parents – Horim - הורים
Why - Mado'a / Lama – מדוע\למה
To say - Lo-mar - לומר
To work - La-avode - לעבוד
I like / I enjoy - (m) Ani o'hev – אני אוהב
I like / I enjoy - (f) Ani o'hevet – אני אוהבת
Something - Ma'shaehu - משהו
Who – Me - מי
We are - Anachnu אנחנו
Building - Binyan בניין
Doctor - Rofei רופא

We are from Haifa.
Anachnu me chaifa.
אנחנו מחיפה.

Your doctor is in the same building.
Ha rofei shelcha neemtza bei oto binyan.
הרופא שלך נמצא באותו בניין.

I like to be at my house with my parents.
Ani o'hev/o'hevet li-hiyot ba- ba'itt eem ha-horim sheli.
אני אוהב\אוהבת להיות בבית עם ההורים שלי.

Why do I need to say something important?
Madoo'a a'lai lomar mashae'hoo chashoov?
מדוע עליי לומר משהו חשוב?

I am there with him.
Ani sham ee-toe.
אני שם איתו.

I like to work.
Ani o'hev/o'hevet la'avod.
אני אוהב\אוהבת לעבוד.

Who is there?
Me sham?
מי שם?

I will be - Ani he'ye – אני אהיה
Good morning - Boker tov – בוקר טוב
Ready - Moo'chan - מוכנים
Soon / quickly - Bekarov בקרוב
Soon / quickly - Ma'her מהר
Soon / quickly - Bem'hera במהרה
Soon / quickly - behekdem בהקדם
Important – Chashuv - חשוב
Busy - (M) Hasuk - עסוק
Busy - (F) Hasuka - עסוקה
Of – Shel - של
Like this – Kacha - ככה

I am busy, but I will be ready quickly.
Ani hasuk/hasuka, aval ani he'ye muchan/muchana bim'hera.
אני עסוק\עסוקה, אבל אני אהיה מוכן\מכונה במהרה.

I want to know if they are here.
Ani rotzei lada'at eem hem kan.
אני רוצה לדעת אם הם שם.

I can go outside.
Ani yachol latzet hachootza.
אני יכול לצאת החוצה.

There is a taxi outside.
Yesh monit bachutz.
יש מונית בחוץ.

Do it like this!
Tahase'e et ze kach!
תעשה את זה כך!

*This *isn't* a phrase book! The purpose of this book is *solely* to provide you with the tools to create *your own* sentences!

How much, how many — Kama - כמה
To bring - Le-havee - להביא
With me — Iti - איתי
Instead — Bimkom - במקום
Only — Rak - רק
When — Matai - מתי
Were - Ha-yu - היו
Without me - Bi'ladai - בלעדיי
You can — Ata yachol – אתה יכול

Only when you can.
(M)Rak matai shei ata yachol.
רק מתי שאתה יכול.
(F)Rak matai shei ah'tt ye'chola.
רק מתי שאת יכולה.

Go there without me.
Lech lesham bila'da'yee.
לך לשם בלעדיי.

How much money do I need to bring with me?
Kama kesef ani tzarich/tzreicha le-havee ee-tee?
כמה כסף אני צריך\צריכה להביא איתי?

It is already there.
Ze kvar sham.
זה כבר שם.

*With the knowledge you've gained so far, now try to create your own sentences!

Fast - Ma'her - מהר
Slow - Le-at - לאט
Inside – Befnim - בפנים
Cold – Kar - קר
Hot – Cham - חם
To Drive - Linhog לנהוג
To Drive - Lin-so-ah לנסוע
To eat - Le-echol - לאכול
Do I – Ani – אני
Do I? – Haeem ani? – ?האם אני
Lunch – Aruchat hatzo'horaiim – ארוחת הצהריים

I prefer bread instead of rice.
Ani mahadif lechem bimkom orez.
אני מעדיף לחם על אורז.

I need to drive in the car very fast or very slow.
Ani tza'rich/tz'rei'cha linhog ba-mechoniit mei'od ma'her o mei'od
le'at.
אני צריך\צריכה לנהוג במכונית מאוד מהר או מאוד לאט.

It is already there.
Ze kvar sham.
זה כבר שם

This is a good meal.
Zot arucha tova.
זאת ארוחה טובה.

I like to eat a hot meal for my lunch.
Ani o'hev/o'hevet leichol aroocha chama la aroochat hatz'hraym.
אני אוהב\אוהבת לאכול ארוחה חמה לארוחת הצהריים.

The winter is very cold in Israel.
Hachoref kar meihod be'israel
החורף קר מאוד בישראל.

To answer - La-anote - לענות
To fly - La-toos - לטוס
To travel – Letayel - לטייל
To learn – Lilmod - ללמוד
How – Eich - איך
To leave - Le-hasheer - להשאיר
Time - Pa-am - פעם
United States - hartzot habrit ארצות הברית
Hill - Giv'ah גיבעה
Mountain - Haar הר

Since the first time.
Meaz ha pa'am ha-rishona.
.מאז הפעם הראשונה

The children are yours!
Ha yeladim shelcha!
!הילדים שלך

I need to answer many questions.
Ani tza'rich/tz'rei'cha la'anote al harbei shaei'lot.
אני צריך\צריכה לענות על הרבה שאלות

I want to fly to the United States today.
Ani rotzeh/rotza la-toos hayom lei hartzot habrit.
.אני רוֹצֶה\רוֹצָה לטוס היום לארצות הברית

Our house is on the hill.
Habait shelanu al hagiv'ah
הבית שלנו על הגבעה

*In Hebrew, to leave (a place) is *la-a-zove* - לעזוב; to leave (an object)
is *le'hasheer* - להשאיר.

To swim – Lischot - לשחות
To practice – Lehitamen - להלחם
To play – Lesachek - לשחק
Our – Shelanu - שלנו
How – Eich - איך
Pool – Brecha - בריכה
First - (M) Rishon- ראשון
First - (F) Rishona - ראשונה
Money – Kesef - כסף
Enough - Maspik מַסְפִּיק

I need to learn how to swim at our pool.
Ani tza'rich/tz'rei'cha lilmod eich lischot ba brecha shelanu.
אני צריך\צריכה ללמוד איך לשחות בבריכה שלנו.

I want to leave my dog at home.
Ani rotzei lahasheer et ha kelev sheli ba ba'yeet.
אני רוצה להשאיר את הכלב שלי בבית.

I want to travel the world.
Ani rotzei letayel ba o'lam.
אני רוצה לטייל בעולם.

I want to learn how to play better tennis.
Ani rotzei lilmod lesachek tennis tov yoter.
אני רוצה ללמוד לשחק טניס טוב יתר.

I don' have enough money.
Ein li maspik kesef.
אין לי מספיק כסף.

That is a very tall mountain.
Ze har gavo'ha meihod.
זה הר גבוה מאוד.

Nobody / anyone - Af echad – אף אחד
Against – Neged - נגד
Us / we / we are - Anach'nu -אנחנו
To visit - Le'vaker – לבקר/
Mom – Ima - אמא
To give - La-tet - לתת/
Just – Rak - רק
You *(indirect object)* **– (m)** Lecha- לְךָ/
You *(indirect object)* **- (f)** Lach - לָךְ *(read footnote below)*
Family – Mishpacha - משפחה
Week – Shavuha - שבוע
Than - Mi מ
Than - Mae'asher מאשר

Something is better than nothing.
Mashaehu ze yoter tov mi kloom.
משהו זה יותר טוב מכלום.

I am against.
Ani neged.
אני נגד

Do you do this everyday?
Ata oseh et ze kol yom?
אתה עושה את זה כל יום?

We go to visit my family each week.
Anachnu holechim/holchot levaker et ha mishpacha sheli kol shavuha.
אנחנו הולכים\הולכות לבקר את המשפחה שלי כל שבוע.

I need to give you something.
Ani tza'rich/tz'rei'cha latet lecha/lach mashehu.
אני צריך\צריכה לתת לְךָ\לָךְ משהו.

Lecha / lach is the indirect object pronoun of the pronoun "you," the person who is actually affected by the action that is being carried out.

Someone - (m) Mi-shehu - מישהו
Someone - (f)mi'she'hee - מישהי
Nothing - Shoom davar – שום דבר
Nothing - Kloom כלום
Each / Every – Kol - כל
Around – Misaviv - מסביב
To walk - La-lechet - ללכת
To meet – Lifgosh - לפגוש
Towards - Likrat לקראת
Towards - Lei'ever לעבר
Five – Chamesh - חמש
Minute - Daka דקה
Minutes - Dakot – דקות

Do you want to meet someone?
Haiim ata rotzeh/rotza lifgosh mi-shehu?
?האם אתה רוֹצֶה\רוֹצָה לפגוש מישהו

I am here tomorrow as well.
Ani poe gam machar.
.אני פה גם מחר

You need to walk around the school.
Ata tzarich / att tzreicha lalechet misaviv la beit ha sefer.
.אתה צריך\את צריכה ללכת מסביב לבית הספר

From here to there, it's just five minutes.
Mi poe le-sham, ze rak chamesh dakot.
.מפה לשם, זה רק חמש דקות

*In Hebrew, you use *haiim* - האם? whenever asking a question, starting with "do," "does," "are," etc., for example:
* "do you…?" / *haiim ata / ah'tt?* את \ האם אתה?
* "does he, she…?" / *haiim hu? / hee?* היא\האם הוא?
* "does the…?" / *haiim ha?* ה האם…?
* "are they…?" / *haiim hem?* האם הם?
* "is it possible…?" / *haiim ze efshari?* האם זה אפשרי?

31

I have - Yesh li – יש לי
I don't have - Ein li – אין לי
To borrow - Le-hash'ill - להשאיל
To borrow - Lilvot לילוות
To Loan - Le-alvot להלוות
Grandfather – Saba - סבא
To want – Lirtzot - לרצות
To stay - Le-hish-a-er - להשאר
To continue - Le-hamshich - להמשיך
To show - Le-harot - להראות
Way – Derech - דרך
School - Beit sefer בית ספר
Located - Memukam ממוקם
Located - Nimtza נמצא
Mall - Kenyon קניון
On / about – Al - על

Why don't you have the book?
Lama ein lecha/lach et ha-sefer?
למה אין לְךָ \ לָךְ את הספר?

I want to borrow this book for my grandfather.
Ani rotze le-hash'ill et ha sefer ha ze bishvil saba sheli.
אני רוצה להשאיל את הספר הזה בשביל סבא שלי.

Can you show me the way to the Western Wall?
Ata yachol laharot li et ha-derech la kotel?
אתה יכול להראות לי את הדרך לכותל?

I want to stay in Tel-Aviv because I have a friend there.
Ani rotzei/rotza le'hisha'er bae tel-aviv kee yesh li sham chaver.
אני רוֹצֶה\רוֹצָה להשאר בתל אביב כי יש לי שם חבר.

The school is located near the mall.
Beit ha-sefer memukam leyad ha-kenyon.
בית הספר ממוקם ליד הקניון.

To look like - Le'hiraot kmo – כמו להראות
To prepare - Le-hit-konen - להתכונן
Like (preposition) – Kmo - כמו
Friend – Chaver - חבר
Man - Ish איש
Man - Gever גבר
Woman - Isha אישה
Woman - Geveret גברת
Breakfast - Aruchat boker – בוקר ארוחת
That's why – Lachen - לכן
To show - Le-harot - להראות
With you - **(male)**Itch'a - אִתְּךָ
With you - **(female)**It'ach - אִתָּךְ

Do you want to look like a Matan?
Haiim ata/ah'tt rotze/rotza le'hiraot kmo Matan?
?האם אתה\את רוֹצֶה\רוֹצָה להראות כמו מתן

I want to drive and to continue on this way to my house.
Ani rotze lin-so-ah ve le-hamshich ba-derech hazot la-ba'itt sheli.
.אני רוצה לנסוע ולהמשיך בדרך הזאת לבית שלי

I need to show you how to prepare breakfast.
Ani tza'rich/tz'rei'cha le-harote lecha/lach eich le-hachin aruchat boker.
.אני צריך\צריכה להראות לְךָ\ לָךְ איך להכין ארוחת בוקר

I don't need the car today.
Ani lo tza'rich/tz'rei'cha et ha-mechoniit ha-yom.
.אני לֹא צריך\צריכה את המכונית היום

I want to come with you.
Ani rotze/rotza lavo itach/ itcha.
.אני רוצה לבוא איתך

To remember - Li-zkor - לזכור
Your – (m) Shelcha - שלך
Your – (f) Shelach - שלך
Number – Mispar - מספר
Hour - Sha-ah - שעה
Dark - Choshech חושך
Darkness - Chashecha – חשיכה
Grandmother – Safta - סבתא
More - Yoterיותר
More - Ode עוד
To think - Lach-shove - לחשוב
To hear - Li-shmoa - לשמוע
To listen - Le-haziin להאזין
To listen - Le-akshiiv להקשיב
Last - (m) Acharon - אחרון
Last - (f) Acharona - אחרונה
To speak / to talk – Ledaber - לדבר
To do - La-a-sote - לעשות
A second - Shnee'ya - שנייה

You need to remember your number.
Atta/ah'tt tza'rich/tz'rei'cha li-zkor et ha-mispar shelcha/shelach.
אתה\את צריך\צריכה לזכור את המספר שֶׁלְּךָ\שֶׁלָּךְ.

This is the last hour of darkness.
Zot ha-sha-ah ha'acharona shel ha chashecha.
זאת השעה האחרונה של החשיכה.

I can hear my grandmother speaking Hebrew.
Ani yachol/yechola lishmo'a et ha savta sheli medaberet ivrit.
אני יכול\יכולה לשמוע את הסבתא שלי מדברת עברית.

I need to think about this more.
Ani tzarich lachshov a'al ze yoter.
אני צריך לחשוב על זה יותר.

Conversational Hebrew Quick and Easy

To leave - La-a-zove - לעזוב
Again - Shuv שוב
Again - Ode pa'am – עוד פעם
To take – Lakachat - לקחת
To try – Lenasot - לנסות
To rent - Le-ha-zkir - להשכיר
To rent - Lizchor לשכור
To ask - Le-vakesh - לבקש
To stop – Lehafsik - להפסיק
To turn off – Lechabot - לכבות
Beach - Chof hayam – חוף הים

I need to rent a house on the beach.
Ani tza'rich/tz'rei'cha le-ha-zkir ba'itt al chof hayam.
אני צריך\צריכה לשכורבית על חוף הים.

I want to take this with me.
Ani rotze/rotza lakachat et ze iti.
אני רוצֶה\רוצָה לקחת את זה איתי.

We want to stop here.
Anachnu rotzim/rotzot la'aatzor poe.
אנחנו רוצים\רוצות לעצור פה.

I need to turn off the lights early.
Ani tzarich/tzreicha lechabot et ha orot mukdam.
אני צריך\צריכה לכבות את האור מוקדם.

Is this for me?
Haiim ze bishvili?
האם זה בשבילי?

Lehafsik – לפסיק is "to cease," and *lahatzor* – לעצור is "to physically stop," for example, "to stop the car" / *lahatzor et ha'mechoniit* – לעצור את המכונית.

*The definition of *chof hayam* – חוף הים is "beach." But the literal definition is "shore of the sea": *chof* - חוף ("shore") *hayam* - הים("of the sea").

The Program

To open - Lifto-ach - לפתוח
A bit, a little, a little bit – Ktzat קצת
A bit, a little, a little bit – Mae'at מעט
Sister – Achot - אחות
Nice to meet you - (m) Naiim lahakir otach נעים להכיר אותך
Nice to meet you - (f) Naiim lahakir otcha נעים להכיר אותך
To buy - Liknot לקנות
Something - Mashae'hu משהו
Something - Davar דבר
Name – Shem - שם
Last name - Shem mishpacha – שם משפחה
Door - De-let - דלת
There isn't/ there aren't – Ein אין
Early – Mukdam - מוקדם

I need to open the door for my sister.
Ani tza'rich/tz'rei'cha liftoach et ha de-let bishvil achot'ee.
אני צריך\צריכה לפתוח את הדלת בשביל אחותי.

I need to buy something.
Ani tza'rich/tz'rei'cha liknot mashaehu.
אני צריך\צריכה לקנות משהו.

I want to meet your brothers.
Ani rotzei lifgosh et ha acheem shelcha.
אני רוצה לפגוש את האחים שלך.

Nice to meet you. What is your name and your last name?
Naiim lehakir otcha/otach. Ma hashem shelcha/shelach ve shem ha mishpacha?
נעים לכיר אותך\אותך. מה השם שֶׁלְּךָ\שֶׁלָּךְ והשם משפחה?

*With the knowledge you've gained so far, now try to create your own sentences!

To live (to exist) - Li-chiyot - לחיות
To live (in a place) - Lagoor לגור
To return - La-cha-zor - לחזור
To hope – Lekavot - לקוות
Without - B'lee - בלי
Hebrew – Ivrit - עברית
Synagogue - Beit knesset בית כנסת
Sad - (M) Atzov - עצוב
Sad - (F)atzova - עצובה

We can hope for a better future.
Anoo yecholeem lekavot le a'ateed tov yoter.
אנו יכולים לקוות לעתיד טוב יותר.

It is impossible to live without problems.
Yee efshar leechyot blee bae'ayot.
אי אפשר לחיות בלי בעיות.

I want to return to the United States.
Ani rotzei/rotza lachzor lei artzot ha breet.
אני רוֹצֶה\רוֹצָה לחזור לארצות הברית.

Why are you sad right now?
Lama ata/ah'tt atzov/atzova achshav?
למה אתה\את עצוב\עצובה עכשיו?

   *In the Hebrew language, pronouns become suffixes to the noun, although it isn't incorrect to say *achot shelcha* – אחות שלך. For example:

   *   "sister" / *achot* - אחות
   *   "my sister" / *achot'ee* - אחותי
   *   "your sister" / *achot'cha* - אחותך
   *   "her sister" / *achota* - אחותה
   *   "his sister" / *achoto* - אחותו
   *   "their sister" / *achotam* - אחותם
   *   "our sister" / *achotainu* - אחותינו

To happen - Li-krote - לקרות
To order - Le-hazmeen - להזמין
To drink – Lishtote - לשתות
To keep – Lishmor - לשמור
To begin / to start - Le-hatchil - להתחיל
To finish – Ligmor - לגמור
Child -(m) Yeled - ילד
Child (f) Yalda - ילדה
Child (plural-m) Yeladim - ילדים
Child (plural-f) Yeladot - ילדות
Woman – Isha - אישה
Excuse me / sorry – Slicha - סליחה

This needs to happen today.
Zeh tza'rich likrote ha yom.
זה צריך לקרות היום.

My child he is here as well.
Ha yeled sheli gam poe.
הילד שלי גם פה.

I want to order a soup.
Ani rotzei/rotza lehazmeen marak.
אני רוֹצֶה\רוֹצָה להזמין מרק.

We want to start the class soon.
Anoo rotzeem lehatcheel et ha shee'oor baehekdem.
אנו רוצים להתחיל את השיעור בהקדם

In order to finish at three o'clock this afternoon, I need to finish soon
Kedei lesayem bae shalosh achar ha tzoharaeem, ani tzarich/tzreicha lesayem be'ekdem.
כדי לסיים בשלוש אחר הצהריים, אני צריך\צריכה לסיים בהקדם.

To speak / to talk – Ledaber - לדבר
To help - La-azore - לעזור
To smoke - Le'aashen - לעשן
To love / to like - Le-ehove - לאהוב
How – Eich - איך

I want to learn how to speak Hebrew fluently.
Ani rotzei/rotza lilmod eich ledaber ivrit shotefet.
אני רוֹצֶה\רוֹצָה ללמוד איך לדבר עברית שוטפת.

I don't want to smoke again.
Ani lo rotze/rotza le'aashen shuv.
אני לא רוֹצֶה\רוֹצָה לעשן שוב.

I want to help.
Ani rotze/rotza la'aazor.
אני רוֹצֶה\רוֹצָה לעזור.

I love you.
Ani ohev/ohevet otcha/otach.
אני אוהב\אוהבת אוֹתְךָ\אוֹתָךְ.

I see you.
Ani ro'eh/ro'ha otcha/otach.
אני רוֹאֶה\רוֹאָה אוֹתְךָ\אוֹתָךְ.

I need you.
Ani tzarich/tzraicha otcha/otach.
אני צריך\צריכה אוֹתְךָ\אוֹתָךְ.

Otcha / otach - אוֹתְךָ\אוֹתָךְ is the direct object pronoun of the pronoun "you." *The definition of "child" is *(M)Yeled* - ילד/ *(f)yalda - ילדה* however the plural forms are *(p-m)yeladim* - ילדים/ *(p-f)yeladot - ילדות*.

39

To read – Likro - לקרוא
To write – Lichtov - לכתוב
To teach – Lelamed - ללמד
To close – Lisgor - לסגור
To choose - Livchor לבחור
To prefer - Le'aadif - להעדיף
To put - La-seem - לשים
Less – Pachot - פחות
Sun – Shemesh - שמש
Month – Chodesh - חודש
Permission - Ri-shote - רשות
Exact - Medu'yak מְדוּיָק
Airport - Sdei tehufa שדה תעופה
To sleep - Lishon לישון

In order to leave you have to ask permission.
Kedei lahazov ata chayav/att chayevet levakesh reshoot.
כדי לעזוב אתה חייב \ את חייבת לבקש רשות.

I want to go to sleep now because I need to wake up early in order to take a taxi to the airport.
Ani tzarich/tzraicha lalechet lishon achshav biglal shae ani tzarich/traicha leitorer mukdam kedei lakachat monit lezdei-hatae'oofa.
אני צריך\צריכה ללכת לישון עכשיו בגלל שאני צריך\תריכה להתעורר מוקדם כדי לקחת מונית לשדה תעופה.

Is it possible to know the exact date of the flight?
Haiim ze efshari lada'aat et ha ta-arich ha meduyak shel ha'tissa?
האם זה אפשרי לדעת את התאריך המדויק של הטיסה?

I need this book to learn how to read and write in Hebrew.
Ani tzarich/tzreicha lilmod eich likro ve lichtov bei/ivrit.
אני צריך\צריכה ללמוד איך לקרוא ולכתוב בעברית.

I want to teach English in Israel.
Ani rotzei/rotza lelamed anglit bei yees'ra'el.
אני רוֹצֶה\רוֹצָה ללמד אנגלית בישראל.

To turn on – Lehadlik - להדליק
In order – Kedei - כדי
Date – Taharich - תאריך
Possible – Efshari - אפשרי
Exact – Meduyak - מדויק
I talk / I am talking - (m) Ani Medaber – אני מדבר
I talk / I am talking - (f) Ani Medaberet – אני מדברת

I want to turn on the lights and close the door.
Ani rotzei lahadleek ha orot ve lisgor et ha delet.
אני רוצה להדליק את האורות ולסגור את הדלת.

I need to go outside.
Ani tzarich/tzreicha latzet ha'chutza.
אני צריך\צריכה לצאת החוצה.

Is it possible to know the exact date of the flight?
Haiim ze efshari lada'aat et ha ta-arich ha meduyak shel ha'tissa?
האם זה אפשרי לדעת את התאריך המדויק של הטיסה?

I talk with the boy and with the girl in English.
Ani medaber/medaberet eim ha-yeled ve eim ha-yalda be anglit.
אני מדבר\מדברת עם הילד ועם הילדה באנגלית.

I want to pay less than you.
Ani rotzei leshalem pachot mimcha.
אני רוצה לשלם פחות ממך.

I prefer to put this here.
Ani ma'adeef laseem et zei kan.
אני מעדיף לשים את זה כאן.

*The definition of "than" is *mi* – מ.... (However, when combined with a pronoun, it becomes a prefix). For example:
* "than you" / *mimcha* – ממך.
* "than me" / *mimeni* – ממני.
* "than him" / *mimeno* – ממנו.
* "than her" / *mimena* – ממנה.
* "than us" / *me'itanu* – מאיתנו.

Up – Lemaala - למעלה
Down – Lemata - למטה
Below, under – Mitachat - מתחת
Above - Mae'al מעל
Of course - Behechlet בהחלט
Of course - be'vadai – בוודאי
To follow - La-a-kove - לעקוב
New – Chadash -חדש
To arrive - Le'hag'ee'aa - להגיע
Theater - Te'atron - תאטרון
Welcome - Bruchim habaiim – ברוכים הבאים
Dog - Kelev כלב

Of course I can come to the theater, and I want to sit together with you and your family.
Bevadai sheh ani yachol/ye'chola lehag'ee'aa la-te'atron, ve ani rotze/rotza lashevet beyachad itcha/itach ve im ha mishpacha shelcha.
בוודאי שאני יכול\יכולה להגיע לתאטרון, ואני רוצה\רוצה לשבת ביחד איתך\איתָך ועם המשפחה שלך

If you look under the table, you can see the new rug.
Eem tistakel mitachat lashoolchan, ata tochal lirot et ha marvad ha chadash.
אם תסתכל מתחת לשולחן, אתה תוכל לראות את מרבד החדש.

I can see the sky from the window.
Ani yachol lirot et ha shamayim me'hachalon.
אני יכול לראות את השמיים מהחלון.

The dog wants to follow me to the store.
Ha kelev rotzei lahakov achar'a'ee la chanoot.
הכלב רוצה לעקוב אחרי לחנות.

*In Hebrew "to call (on the phone)" is *lehitkasher* - להתקשר. However, to call out to someone is *likro* - לקרוא.

To allow - Le-harshot - להרשות
To believe - Leha'amin - להאמין
To promise - Le-havtiach - להבטיח
To recognize – Lehakir - להכיר
People – Anashim - אנשים
Far – Rachok - רחוק
Him - Lo לו / **Her** - La לה
Morning - Boker בוקר
Good night - Laila tov – לילה טוב
Except – Milvad - מלבד
So (as in *then*) – Az - אז
So (as in *so much*) - Kol-kach – כל כך

I need to allow him to go with us.
Ani tzareech laharshot lo la lechet eetan'oo.
אני צריך להרשות לו ללכת איתנו.

I can't recognize him.
Ani lo yachol lahakeer oto.
אני לא יכול להכיר אותו.

Come here quickly.
Bo lekan ma'her.
בוא הנה מהר

I need to believe everything except for this.
Ani tza'rich/tz'rei'cha le'ha'amin le'ha-kol milvad zeh.
אני צריך\צריכה להאמין להכל מלבד זה.

I must promise myself not to forget to say good night to my parents each night.
Ani chayav/chyevet le-havtiach le'atzmi lo lishkoach lomar Laila tov la'horim sheli behchol laila.
אני חייב\חייבת להבטיח לעצמי לא לשכוח לומר לילה טוב להורים שלי בכל לילה.

So why is this so small?
Az lama ze kol-kach katan?
אז למה זה כל כך קטן?

Man - Ish איש
To enter - Le-hikanes - להיכנס
To receive – Lekabel - לקבל
To move (to a place) - La-avore - לעבור
To move (an object) - La-aziz להזיז
Left - Smol שמאל
Right - Yamin ימין
Each / every - Kol כל
Good afternoon - Tza-haraim tovim – צהריים טובים
Different - Acher אחר
Different - shoneh שונה
Throughout - Beh'meshech - בהמשך
Through – Derech - דרך

He is a different man now.
Hoo eesh acher achshav.
הוא איש אחר עכשיו.

I need to move my car because my sister needs to move her things to her car
Ani tza'rich/tz'rei'cha la-aziz et ha mechonit sheli biglal shae achoti tzreicha la-havir et ha-dvarim shela lamechonit shela.
אני צריך\צריכה להזיז את המכונית שלי בגלל שאחותי צריכה להעביר את הדברים שלה למכונית שלה.

I see the sun from the kitchen window throughout the morning.
Ani ro'eh/ro'ha et hashemesh me'chalon ha mitbach bemieshech ha'boker.
אני רוֹאֶה\רוֹאָה את השמש מחלון המטבח במשך הבוקר.

I go into the house from the front entrance and not through the yard.
Ani nichnas la ba'eet mee ha kneesa ha keedmeet ve lo derech ha chatzcr.
אני נכנס לבית מהכניסה הקדמית ולא דרך החצר.

44

To wish - Le'achel - לאחל
Bad – Rah - רע
To get - Lekabel / Lakachat – לקבל\לקחת
To forget – Lishkoach - לשכוח
Everybody – Kulam - כולם
Although – Lamrot - למרות
In front – Lifnei - לפני
To exchange - Le hachlif - להחליף
To change – Leshanot - לשנות
To call – Likro - לקרוא
To sit – Lashevet - לשבת
Brother – Ach - אח
Dad – Aba - אבא
Together – Beyachad - ביחד
Years – Shanim - שנים
Big – Gadol - גדול
Never - Le'olam - לעולם
During – Bezman בזמן

I want to exchange the money at the bank.
Ani rotze le-hachlif et hakesef ba-bank.
אני רוצה להחליף את הכסף בבנק.

I want to call my brother and my dad today.
Ani rotzeh/rotza lehitkasher le-ach sheli ve le-aba sheli hayom.
אני רוצֶה\רוצָה להתקשר לאח שלי ולאבא שלי היום.

I don't ever want to see you.
Ani le'olam lo rotze lirot otcha.
אני לעולם לא רוצה לראות אותך.

I don't want to wish you anything bad.
Ani lo rotzeh/rotza le'achel lecha mashehu ra'aa.
אני לא רוצֶה\רוצָה לאחל לך משהו רע.

I must forget everybody from my past.
Ani chayav/chayevet lishko'ach et koolam mei ha avar.
אני חייב\חייבת לשכוח את כולם מהעבר.

Next (following/after) - Ha'ba - הבא
Next (near/close) - Karov, קרוב
Next (near/close) - Le-yad – ליד
Behind - Me-achor - מאחור
Restaurant - Mis'aada - מסעדה
Bathroom - Shirut-im - שירותים
Bathroom - Chadar ambatya בחדר אמבטיה
See you soon / goodbye - Lehit-raot - להתראות
I must - Ani Chayav – אני חייב
Person - Adaam אדם
Person - Ben adaam בן אדם
Good – Tov - טוב
Which – Eizei - איזה
Area - Ezor איזור
Area - Sviva סביבה

Goodbye my friend.
Leihit'ra'ot chaver.
להתראות חבר.

Which is the best restaurant in the area?
Eezo misada achi tova ba sviva.
איזו מסעדה הכי טובה בסביבה?

I can feel the heat.
Ani yachol lahargeesh et ha chom.
אני יכול להרגיש את החום.

She must get a car before the next year.
Hee tzreicha lekabel mechoniit lifnei ha shana ha'ba'aa.
היא צריכה לקבל מכונית לפני השנה הבאה.

I need to repair a part of the cabinet in the bathroom.
Ani tzarich letaken chelek mei aron ba chadar ambatya.
אני צריך לתקן חלק מהארון בחדר אמבטיה.

Please – Bevakasha - בבקשה
Beautiful - (m)Yafeh - יָפֶה,
Beautiful - (f)yafa - יָפָה
To lift - Le-harim - להרים
Include / Including – Kolel - כולל
Belong – Shayach - שייך
To check – Livdok - לבדוק
Small – Katan - קטן
To feel – Lahargish - להרגיש
Sorry – Slicha - סליחה

I am sorry.
Ani mitzta'er.
אני מצטער

To feel well I must take vitamins.
Kedei lahargeesh tov alai lakachat veetameen'eem.
כדי להרגיש טוב עליי לקחת ויטמינים.

I am near the person that's behind you.
Ani karov l'adam sheh me-achorei'cha/me-achoraeich.
אני קרוב לאדם מֵאֲחוֹרֶיךָ \ מֵאֲחוֹרַיִךְ.

We need to check the size of the house.
Anachnu tz'reichim livdok et godel ha-ba'itt.
אנחנו צריכים לבדוק את גודל הבית.

I want to lift this.
Ani rotzei lehareem et zei.
אני רוצה להרים את זה.

Can you please put the wood in the fire?
Ata yachol laseem et ha etz ba'esh?
אתה יכול לשים את העץ באש?

Does the price include everything?
Haiim ha mechir kolel hakol?
האם המחיר כולל הכל?

To hold – Lehachzik - להחזיק
For me – Bishvili - בשבילי
Price – Mechir - מחיר
Real - Amee-tee - אמיתי
Thing – Davar - דבר
Doesn't – Lo - לא
Even though – Lamrot - למרות
Sky – Shamayim - שמיים

Is that a real diamond?
Ha'eem zei yahalom ameet'ee?
?האם זה יהלום אמיתי

This week the weather was very beautiful.
Ha shavua ha-mezeg ha-avir haya mei'od yafeh.
.השבוע מזג האויר היה מאוד יפה

The sun is high in the sky.
Ha shemesh gvoa ba shama'eem.
.השמש גבוה בשמיים

I can pay this although the price is expensive.
Ani yachol leshalem et ze lamrot sheh hamechir gavo'ha.
.אני יכול לשלם את זה למרות שהמחיר גבוה

Can you please hold my hand?
Ata yachol / att yechola lahachzeek lee et ha yad?
?אתה יכול\את יכולה להחזיק את היד

I want to go to sleep.
Ani rotzei/rotza lalechet lishon.
.אני רוֹצֶה\רוֹצָה ללכת לישון

Where is the airport?
Eifo sdei ha te'oofa?
?איפה שדה התעופה

Building Bridges

In Building Bridges, we take six conjugated verbs that have been selected after studies I have conducted for several months in order to determine which verbs are most commonly conjugated, and which are then automatically followed by an infinitive verb. For example, once you know how to say, "I need," "I want," "I can," and "I like," you will be able to connect words and say almost anything you want more correctly and understandably. The following three pages contain these six conjugated verbs in first, second, third, fourth, and fifth person, as well as some sample sentences. Please master the entire program up until *here* prior to venturing onto this section.

I need - (m) Ani tzarich – אני צריך

I need - (f) Ani tz'rei'cha – אני צריכה

I want - (m) Ani rotzeh – אני רוֹצֶה

I want - (f) Ani rotza – אני רוֹצֶה

I have – (m) Yesh li – יש לי

I have – (f) Yesh li – יש לי

I have to / I must - (m) Ani chayav – אני חייב

I have to / I must - (f) Ani cha'yevet – אני חייבת

I talk - (m) Ani medaber – אני מדבר

I talk - (f) Ani medaberet – אני מדברת

I want to go home.
Ani rotzeh/rotza lalechet habayita.
אני רוֹצֶה\רוֹצֶה ללכת הביתה.

I need to find a hospital.
Ani tza'rich/tz'rei'cha limtzo et beit hacholim.
אני צריך\צריכה למצוא את בית החולים.

I need to walk outside the museum.
Ani tzarich lalechet meechootz la mozeihon.
אני צריך ללכת מחוץ למוזיאון.

I am talking with you.
Ani medaber/medaberet itcha/itach.
אני מדבר\מדברת אִתְּךָ\אִתָּךְ.

49

I can - (m)Ani yachol – אני יכול
I can - (f)Ani yechola – אני יכולה
I go - (m)Ani holech – אני הולך
I go - (f)Ani holechet – אני הולכת
I do - (m)Ani oseh – אני עוֹשֶׂה
I do - (f)Ani osa – אני עוֹשֶׂה
I see - (m)Ani ro'eh - אני רוֹאֶה
I see - (f)Ani ro'ha – אני רוֹאָה
I like - (m)Ani o'hev – אני אוהב
I like - (f)Ani o'hevet – אני אוהבת
I say - (m)Ani omer – אני אומר
I say - (f)Ani omeret – אני אומרת

I like to eat oranges.
Ani ohev/ohevet le'echol tapozeem.
אני אוהב\אוהבת לאכול תפוזים.

I can go with you.
Ani yachol/yechola lalechit itcha.
אני יכול\יכולה ללכת איתך.

I am seeing a house today.
Ani ro'eh/ro'ha ba'itt ha-yom.
אני רוֹאֶה\רוֹאָה בית היום.

I am doing this now.
Ani ose/osa et ze achshav.
אני אני עוֹשֶׂה\עוֹשֶׂה את זה עכשיו.

I am saying this now.
Ani omer/omeret et ze achshav.
אני אומר\אומרת את זה עכשיו.

Please master *every* single page up until here prior to attempting the following two pages!

(M)You want / do you want?
Atta rotze / haiim atta rotze?
אתה רוֹצֶה \ האם אתה רוצה?

(F) You want / do you want?
Ah'tt rotza / haiim ah'tt rotza?
את רוֹצֶה \ האם את רוֹצֶה?

He wants / does he want?
Hu rotze / haiim hu rotze?
הוא רוצה \ האם הוא רוצה?

She wants / does she want?
Hee rotza / haiim hee rotza?
היא רוצה \ האם היא רוצה?

(M)We want / do we want?
Anachnu rotzim/ Haiim anachnu rotzim?
אנחנו רוצים \ אם אנחנו רוצים?

(F)We want / do we want?
Anachnu rotzot / Haiim anachnu rotzot?
אנחנו רוצות\האם אנחנו רוצות?

(M)They want / do they want?
Hem rotzim / Haiim hem rotzim?
הם רוצים \ האם הם רוצים?

(F)They want / do they want?
Hen rotzot / Haiim hen rotzot?
הן רוצות \ האם הן רוצות?

(M)You (Plural)want/ do you (Pl) want?
Atem rotzim / Haiim atem rotzim?
אתם רוצים \ האם אתם רוצים?

(F)You (pl) want/ do you (Pl) want?
Aten rotzot / Haiim aten rotzot?
אתן רוצות \ האם אתן רוצות?

(M)You need / do you need?

Atta tzarich / haiim atta tzarich?

אתה צריך \ האם אתה צריך?

(F) You need / do you need?

Ah'tt tzraicha / haiim ah'tt tzraicha?

את צריכה \ האם את צריכה?

He needs / does he need?

Hu tzarich / haiim hu tzarich?

הוא צריך \ האם הוא צריך?

She needs / does she need?

Hee tzraicha / haiim hee tzraicha?

היא צריכה \ האם היא צריכה?

(M)We need / do we need?

Anachnu tzraichim/ Haiim anachnu tzraichim?

אנחנו צריכים \ האם אנחנו צריכים?

(F)We need / do we need?

Anachnu tzraichot / Haiim anachnu tzraichot?

אנחנו צריכות \ האם אנחנו צריכות?

(M)They need / do they need?

Hem tzraichim / Haiim hem tzraichim?

הם צריכים \ האם הם צריכים?

(F)They need / do they need?

Hen tzraichot / Haiim hen tzraichot?

הן צריכות \ האם הן צריכות?

(M)You (Pl)need/ do you (Pl) need?

Atem tzraichim / Haiim atem tzraichim?

אתם צריכים\ האם אתם צריכים?

(F)You (pl)need/ do you (Pl) need?

Aten tzraichot / Haiim aten tzraichot?

אתן צריכות \ האם אתן צריכות?

(M)You can / can you?
Atta yachol / haiim atta yachol?
אתה יכול \ האם אתה יכול?

(F) You can / can you?
Ah'tt yechola / haiim ah'tt yechola?
את יכולה \ האם את יכולה?

He can / can he?
Hu yachol / haiim hu yachol?
הוא יכול \ האם הוא יכול?

She can / can she?
Hee yechola / haiim hee yechola?
היא יכולה \ האם היא יכולה?

(M)We can / can we?
Anachnu yecholim/ Haiim anachnu yecholim?
אנחנו יכולים \ האם אנחנו יכולים?

(F)We can / can we?
Anachnu yecholot / Haiim anachnu yecholot?
אנחנו יכולות \ האם אנחנו יכולות?

(M)They can / can they?
Hem yecholim / Haiim hem yecholim?
הם יכולים \ האם הם יכולים?

(F)They can / can they?
Hen yecholot / Haiim hen yecholot?
הן יכולות \ האם הן יכולות?

(M)You (Pl) can/ can you?
Atem yecholim / Haiim atem yecholim?
אתם יכולים \ האם אתם יכולים?

(F)You (pl) can/ can you?
Aten yecholot / Haiim aten yecholot?
אתן יכולות \ האם אתן יכולות?

(M)You do / do you do?
Atta oseh / haiim atta oseh?
אתה עושה \ האם אתה עושה?

(F) You do / do you do?
Ah'tt osah / haiim ah'tt osah?
את עושה \ האם את עושה?

He does / does he do?
Hu oseh / haiim hu oseh?
הוא עושה \ האם הוא עושה?

She does / does she do?
Hee osah / haiim hee osah?
היא עושה \ האם היא עושה?

(M)We do / do we do?
Anachnu osim/ Haiim anachnu osim?
אנחנו עושים \ האם אנחנו עושים?

(F)We do / do we do?
Anachnu osot / Haiim anachnu osot?
אנחנו עושות \ האם אנחנו עושות?

(M)They do / do they do?
Hem osim / Haiim hem osim?
הם עושים \ האם הם עושים?

(F)They do / do they do?
Hen osot / Haiim hen osot?
הן עושות \ האם הן עושות?

(M)You (Pl) do/ do you (Pl) do?
Atem osim / Haiim atem osim?
אתם עושים \ האם אתם עושים?

(F)You (pl) do/ do you (Pl) do?
Aten osot / Haiim aten osot?
אתן עושות \ האם אתן עושות?

(M)You go / do you go?
Atta holech / haiim atta holech?
אתה הולך \ האם אתה הולך?

(F) You go / do you go?
Ah'tt holechet / haiim ah'tt holechet?
את הולכת \ האם את הולכת?

He goes / does he go?
Hu holech / haiim hu holech?
הוא הולך \ האם הוא הולך?

She goes / does she go?
Hee holechet / haiim hee holechet?
היא הולכת \ האם היא הולכת?

(M)We go / do we go?
Anachnu holchim / Haiim anachnu holchim?
אנחנו הולכים \ האם אנחנו הולכים?

(F)We go / do we go?
Anachnu holchot / Haiim anachnu holchot?
אנחנו הולכות \ האם אנחנו הולכות?

(M)They go / do they go?
Hem holchim / Haiim hem holchim?
הם הולכים \ האם הם הולכים?

(F) They go / do they go?
Hen holchot / Haiim hen holchot?
הן הולכות \ האם הן הולכות?

(M)You (Pl) go/ do you (Pl) go?
Atem holchim / Haiim atem holchim?
אתם הולכם \ האם אתם הולכים?

(F) You (pl) go/ do you (Pl) go?
Aten holchot / Haiim aten holchot?
אתן הולכות \ האם אתן הולכות?

(M)You must / do you have to?
Atta chayav / haiim atta chayav?
אתה חייב \ האם אתה חייב?

(F) You must / do you have to?
Ah'tt chayevet / haiim ah'tt chayevet?
את חייבת \ האם את חייבת?

He must / does he have to?
Hu chayav / haiim hu chayav?
הוא חייב \ האם הוא חייב?

She must / does she have to?
Hee chayevet / haiim hee chayevet?
היא חייבת \ האם היא חייבת?

(M)We must / do we have to?
Anachnu chayavim/ Haiim anachnu chayavim?
אנחנו חייבים \ האם אנחנו חייבם?

(F)We must / do we have to?
Anachnu chayavut / Haiim anachnu chayavut?
אנחנו חייבות \ האם אנחנו חייבות?

(M)They must / do they have to?
Hem chayavim / Haiim hem chayavim?
הם חייבים \ האם הם חייבים?

Do you want to go?
(Male) Haiim atta rotze lalechet?
?האם אתה רוצה ללכת
(Female) Haiim ah'tt rotza lalechet?
?האם את רוצה ללכת

Does he want to fly?
Haiim hu rotze la'oof?
?האם הוא רוצה לעוף

She wants to go to the bus station.
He rotza lalechet le'tachanat ha-otoboos.
היא רוצה ללכת לתחנת האוטובוס.

We want to swim.
(M) Anachnu rotzim lischot.
אנחנו רוצים לשחות.
(F) Anachnu rotzot lischot.
אנחנו רוצות לשחות.

Do they want to run?
(M) Haiim hem rotzim larotz?
?האם הם רוצים לרוץ
(F) Haiim hen rotzot larotz?
?האם הן רוצות לרוץ

Do you need to clean?
Haiim atta tzarich lenakot?
?האם אתה צריך לנקות
Haiim ah'tt tzraicha lenakot?
?האם את צריכה לנקות

She needs to sing a song.
Hee tzraicha lashir shir.
היא צריכה לשיר שיר.

We need to travel.
Anachnu tzrechim letayel.
אנחנו צריכים לטייל.

They don't need to fight.
Hem lo tzraichim lariv.
הם לא צריכים לריב.
Hen lo tzreichot lariv.
הן לא צריכות לריב.

You (plural) need to save your money.
Atemn zreichim lachsoch et ha kesef shelachem.
אתם צריכים לחסוך את הכסף שלהם.
Aten zrei'chot lachsoch ct ha kesef shelachen.
אתן צריכות לחסוך את הכסף שלכן.

Can you hear me?
Haiim ata yachol lishmoh'aa oti?
האם אתה יכול לשמוע אותי?
Haiim ah'tt yechola lishmo'aa oti?
האם את יכולה לשמוע אותי?

He can dance very well.
Hu yachol lirkod mei'od tov.
הוא יכול לרקוד מאוד טוב.

We can go out tonight.
Anachnu yecholim latzet halila.
אנחנו יכולים לצאת הלילה.
Anachnu yecholot latzet halila.
אנחנו יכולות לצאת הלילה.

The fireman can break the door during an emergency.
Bezman cheerom ha kaba'eem yecholeem lishbor et ha delet.
בזמן חירום הכבאים יכולים לשבור את הדלת.

Do you like to eat here?
Haiim atta ohev le'echol poe?
האם אתה אוהב לאכול פה?

We like to stay in the house.
Anachnu o'haveem le'ishaher ba ba'iit.
אנחנו אוהבים להישאר בבית.

They like to cook.
Hem ohavim levashel.
הם אוהבים לבשל.
Hen ohavot levashel.
הן אוהבות לבשל.

You (plural) like to play soccer.
Atem oh'haveem lesachek kadoor reg'el.
אתם אוהבים לשחק כדורגל.

Do you go to the movies on weekends?
Ha eem ata olech / att olechet la kolno'a besofei shavoo'a?
?האם אתה הולך \ את הולכת לחנות בסופי שבוע

He goes /fishing.
Hu holech ladoog.
הוא הולך לדוג.

They go out to eat at a restaurant every day.
Em yotzeem la misada kol yom.
הם יוצאים למסעדה כל יום.

Do you have money?
Haiim yesh lecha kesef?
?האם יש לְךָ כסף
Haiim yesh lach kesef?
?האם יש לָךְ כסף

She must look outside.
Hee chayevet lehistakel hachotza.
היא חייבת להסתכל החוצה.

They have to send the letter.
Hem chayavim lishloach et ha'michtav.
הם חייבים לשלוח את המכתב.

You (plural) have to stand in line.
Atem tzreichim la'amod ba torr.
אתם צריכים לעמוד בתור.

Other Useful Tools in the Hebrew Language

Seasons
Spring – Aviv - אביב
Summer - Kah-yits - קיץ
Autumn – Stav - סתיו
Winter – Choref - חורף

Numbers (Masculine tense)
One – Echad - אחד
Two – Shnaim - שנים
Three – Shlosha - שלושה
Four - Arba'aa - ארבעה
Five – Chamisha - חמישה
Six – Shisha - שישה
Seven - Shiva'aa - שבעה
Eight – Shmona - שְׁמוֹנֶה
Nine - Ti-sha'aa - תשעה
Ten - Aasar'aa - עשרה

One boy - Yeled eichad – ילד אחד
Two boys - Shnaei yeladim – שני ילדים
Three boys - Shlosha yeladim – שלושה ילדים
Four boys - Arba-aa yeladim – ארבעה ילדים
Five boys - Chamisha yeladim – חמישה ילדים
Six boys - Shisha yeladim – שישה ילדים
Seven boys - Shiv'aa yeladim – שבעה ילדים
Eight boys - Shmona yeladim – שְׁמוֹנֶה ילדים
Nine boys - Tish'aa yeladim – תשעה ילדים
Ten boys - Aasara yeladim – עשרה ילדים

Numbers (Feminine tense**)**
One – Achat - אחת
Two – Shtaim - שתיים
Three – Shalosh - שלוש
Four – Arba - ארבע
Five – Chamesh - חמש
Six – Shesh - שש
Seven – Sheva - שבע
Eight – Shmoneh - שְׁמוֹנָה
Nine - Taei-sha - תשע
Ten – Eser - עשר

One girl - Yalda achat – ילדה אחת
Two girls - Shtei yeladot – שתי ילדות
Three girls - Shalosh yeladot – שלוש ילדות
Four girls - Arba yeladot – ארבע ילדות
Five girls - Chamesh yeladot – חמש ילדות
Six girls - Shesh yeladot – שש ילדות
Seven girls - Sheva yeladot – שבע ילדות
Eight girls - Shmoneh yeladot – שְׁמוֹנָה ילדות
Nine girls - Taei-sha yeladot – תשע ילדות
Ten girls - Eser yeladot – עשר ילדות

*In the Hebrew Language, when referring to a single noun, the adjective proceeds the noun, example; "one book", *sefer eichad* – ספר אחד. But in plural, the adjective precedes the noun, for example: "two books", *shnaei sfarim* – שני ספרים. When using numbers as adjectives, the conjugation changes, for example: "six books", won't be *shesh sfarim* – שש ספרים, but rather *shisha sfarim* – שישה ספרים.

Days of the Week
Sunday - Yom rishon – יום ראשון
Monday - Yom Sheni – יום שני
Tuesday - Yom Shlishi – יום שלישי
Wednesday - Yom re -ve -ii – יום רביעי
Thursday - Yom Chami shi – יום חמישי
Friday - Yom Shishi – יום שישי
Saturday - Yom Shabat – יום שבת

Colors
Black – Shachor - שחור
White – Lavan - לבן
Gray – A'for - אפור
Red – Adom - אדום
Blue – Kachol - כחול
Yellow - Tsa-hov - צהוב
Green – Yarok - ירוק
Orange – Katom - כתום
Purple – Sagol - סגול
Brown – Chum חום

Cardinal Directions
North – Tzafon - צפון
South – Darom - דרום
East – Mizrach - מזרח
West - Ma'arav - מערב

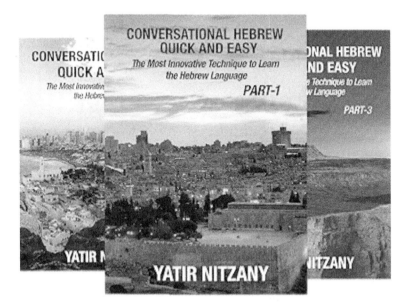

If you enjoyed this book however missed Part-2 and Part-3 then feel free to check them out on Amazon.

NOTE FROM THE AUTHOR

Thank you for your interest in my work. I encourage you to share your overall experience of this book by posting a review. Your review can make a difference! Please feel free to describe how you benefited from my method or provide creative feedback on how I can improve this program. I am constantly seeking ways to enhance the quality of this product, based on personal testimonials and suggestions from individuals like you.

Thanks and best of luck,

Yatir Nitzany

Also by Yatir Nitzany

Conversational Spanish Quick and Easy

....

Conversational French Quick and Easy

....

Conversational Italian Quick and Easy

....

Conversational Portuguese Quick and Easy

....

Conversational German Quick and Easy

....

Conversational Dutch Quick and Easy

....

Conversational Norwegian Quick and Easy

....

Conversational Danish Quick and Easy

....

Conversational Russian Quick and Easy

....

Conversational Ukrainian Quick and Easy

....

Conversational Bulgarian Quick and Easy

....

Conversational Polish Quick and Easy

....

Conversational Hebrew Quick and Easy

....

Conversational Yiddish Quick and Easy

....

Conversational Armenian Quick and Easy

....

Conversational Romanian Quick and Easy

....

Conversational Arabic Quick and Easy

....

Conversational Arabic Quick and Easy
Lebanese Dialect

....

Conversational Arabic Quick and Easy
Syrian Dialect

....

Conversational Arabic Quick and Easy
Jordanian Dialect

....

Conversational Arabic Quick and Easy
Egyptian Dialect

....

Conversational Arabic Quick and Easy
Moroccan Dialect

....

Conversational Arabic Quick and Easy
Tunisian Dialect

....

Conversational Arabic Quick and Easy
Saudi (Hejazi, Najdi & Gulf) Dialect

....

Conversational Arabic Quick and Easy
Iraqi Dialect

....

Conversational Arabic Quick and Easy
Emirati Dialect

....

Conversational Arabic Quick and Easy
Qatari Dialect

....

Conversational Arabic Quick and Easy
Kuwaiti Dialect

Printed in Great Britain
by Amazon

49135265R00040